365 BIBLE PROMISES

STILLWATER GIFTS

Tyndale House Publishers, Inc.
Wheaton, Illinois

Tyndale House Publishers, Inc.
Wheaton, Illinois

Stillwater is a trademark of Tyndale House Publishers, Inc. *Inspirations* is a registered trademark of Tyndale House Publishers, Inc. Scripture quotations marked TLB are taken from *The Living Bible,* copyright © 1971. Used by permission of Tyndale House Publishers, Inc., Wheaton, Illinois 60189. All rights reserved. Scripture quotations marked NIV are from the *Holy Bible,* New International Version®. NIV®. Copyright © 1973, 1978, 1984 by International Bible Society. Used by permission of Zondervan Publishing House. All rights reserved. Scripture quotations marked KJV are taken from the *Holy Bible,* King James Version. Bible clues and answers are from People and Places in the Book game, copyright © 1986 by Tyndale House Publishers, Inc. This calendar was originally published under the titles The Book Calendar and The New 365 Bible Verses Calendar. ■ First printing, July 1993. ISBN 0-8423-3734-2. Copyright © 1993, 1994 by Tyndale House Publishers, Inc. All rights reserved. Cover photo copyright © 1997 by FPG/Miguel S. Salmeron. All rights reserved. No part of this calendar may be reproduced in any manner except by permission of Tyndale House Publishers, Inc. Printed in Singapore

Visit Tyndale's exciting Web site at www.tyndale.com

May the words of my mouth and the meditation of my heart be pleasing in your sight, O LORD, my Rock and my Redeemer.

Psalm 19:14 NIV

JANUARY

New Year's Day

Set your minds on things above, not on earthly things.

Colossians 3:2 NIV

31

December

No one can serve two masters. Either he will hate the one and love the other, or he will be devoted to the one and despise the other. You cannot serve both God and Money.

Matthew 6:24 NIV

JANUARY 2

Thou art worthy, O Lord, to receive glory and honour and power: for thou hast created all things, and for thy pleasure they are and were created.

Revelation 4:11 KJV

DECEMBER 30

I waited patiently for God to help me; then he listened and heard my cry. He lifted me out of the pit of despair.

Psalm 40:1-2 TLB

3 JANUARY

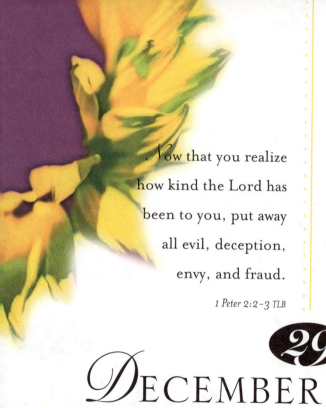

Now that you realize how kind the Lord has been to you, put away all evil, deception, envy, and fraud.

1 Peter 2:2–3 TLB

December 29

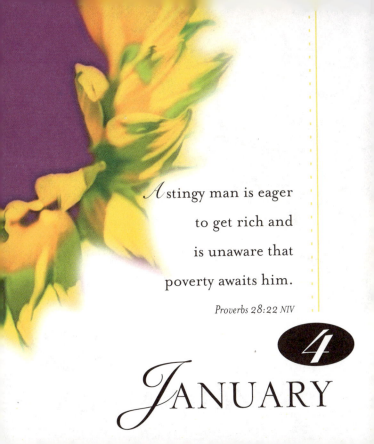

A stingy man is eager to get rich and is unaware that poverty awaits him.

Proverbs 28:22 NIV

4
JANUARY

Give thanks to the LORD, call on his name; make known among the nations what he has done.

Psalm 105:1 NIV

28
DECEMBER

Mercy, peace and love be yours in abundance.

Jude 1:2 NIV

JANUARY 5

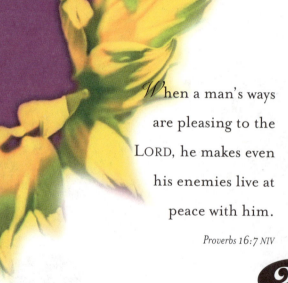

When a man's ways are pleasing to the LORD, he makes even his enemies live at peace with him.

Proverbs 16:7 NIV

27
DECEMBER

How hard it is for those who trust in riches to enter the Kingdom of God.

Mark 10:24 TLB

6
JANUARY

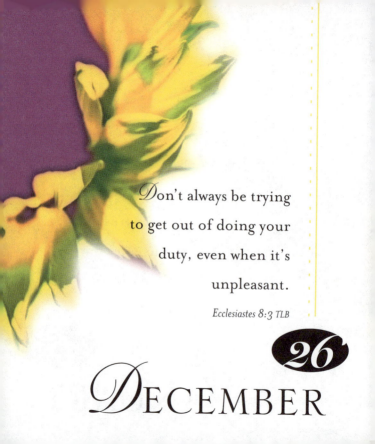

> Don't always be trying to get out of doing your duty, even when it's unpleasant.
>
> *Ecclesiastes 8:3* TLB

DECEMBER 26

*W*isdom brightens a man's face and changes its hard appearance.

Ecclesiastes 8:1 NIV

JANUARY 7

I bring you good news of great joy that will be for all the people. Today in the town of David a Savior has been born to you; he is Christ the Lord.

Luke 2:10-11 NIV

25 DECEMBER

Christmas Day

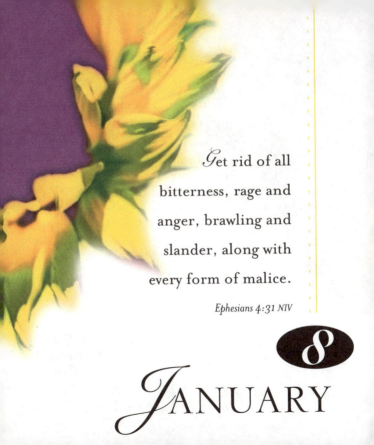

Get rid of all bitterness, rage and anger, brawling and slander, along with every form of malice.

Ephesians 4:31 NIV

8

JANUARY

For unto us a child is born, . . . and his name shall be called Wonderful, Counsellor, The mighty God, The everlasting Father, The Prince of Peace.

Isaiah 9:6 KJV

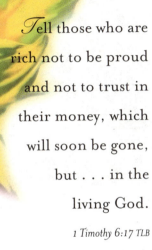

*T*ell those who are rich not to be proud and not to trust in their money, which will soon be gone, but . . . in the living God.

1 Timothy 6:17 TLB

9

JANUARY

Many women do noble things, but you surpass them all.

Proverbs 31:29 NIV

23 DECEMBER

> Faith that does not result in good deeds is not real faith.
>
> *James 2:20 TLB*

January 10

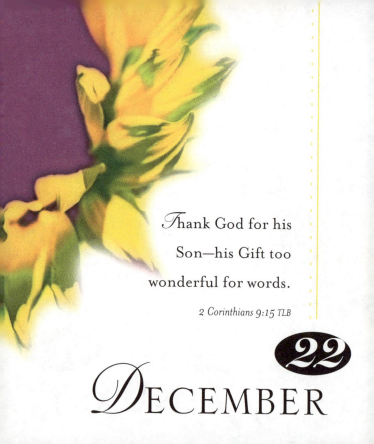

Thank God for his Son—his Gift too wonderful for words.

2 Corinthians 9:15 TLB

DECEMBER 22

Commit to the LORD
whatever you do, and
your plans will succeed.

Proverbs 16:3 NIV

11
JANUARY

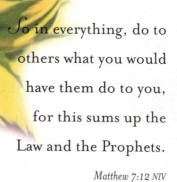

So in everything, do to others what you would have them do to you, for this sums up the Law and the Prophets.

Matthew 7:12 NIV

21

DECEMBER

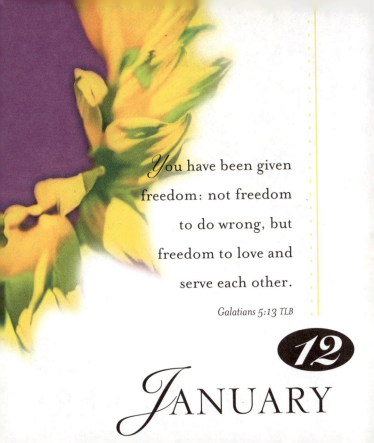

You have been given freedom: not freedom to do wrong, but freedom to love and serve each other.

Galatians 5:13 TLB

12 JANUARY

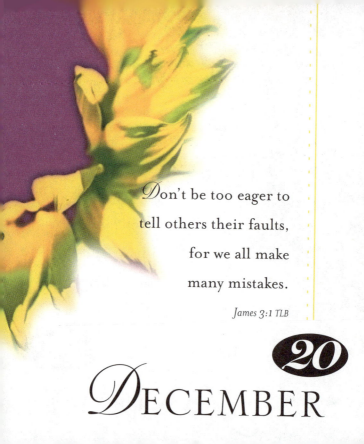

Don't be too eager to tell others their faults, for we all make many mistakes.

James 3:1 TLB

20
DECEMBER

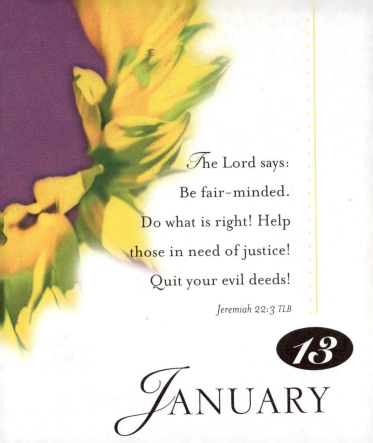

The Lord says: Be fair-minded. Do what is right! Help those in need of justice! Quit your evil deeds!

Jeremiah 22:3 TLB

13
JANUARY

Be kind and compassionate to one another, forgiving each other, just as in Christ God forgave you.

Ephesians 4:32 NIV

19

DECEMBER

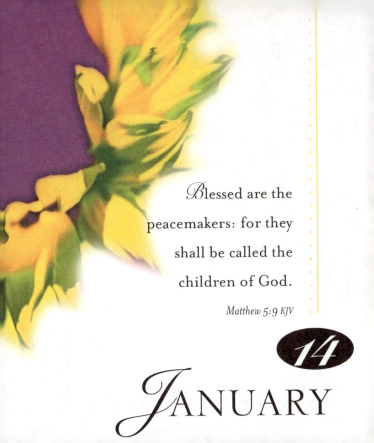

Blessed are the peacemakers: for they shall be called the children of God.

Matthew 5:9 KJV

14 JANUARY

Who may stand before the Lord? Only those with pure hands and hearts, who do not practice dishonesty and lying.

Psalm 24:3-4 TLB

DECEMBER 18

> You have no right to criticize your brother or look down on him. . . . Each of us will give an account of himself to God.
>
> *Romans 14:10, 12 TLB*

15
JANUARY

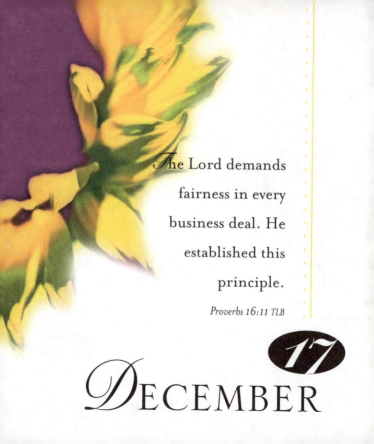

The Lord demands fairness in every business deal. He established this principle.

Proverbs 16:11 TLB

December 17

Let no debt remain outstanding, except the continuing debt to love one another.

Romans 13:8 NIV

JANUARY 16

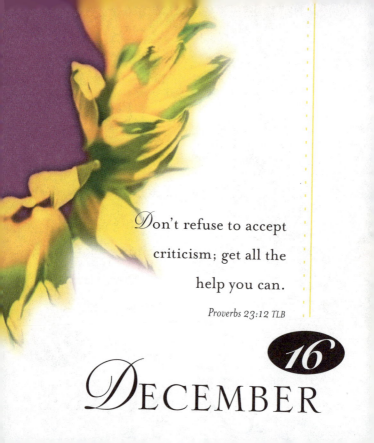

Don't refuse to accept criticism; get all the help you can.

Proverbs 23:12 TLB

DECEMBER 16

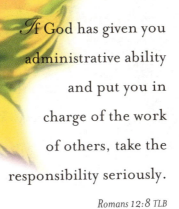

If God has given you administrative ability and put you in charge of the work of others, take the responsibility seriously.

Romans 12:8 TLB

17
JANUARY

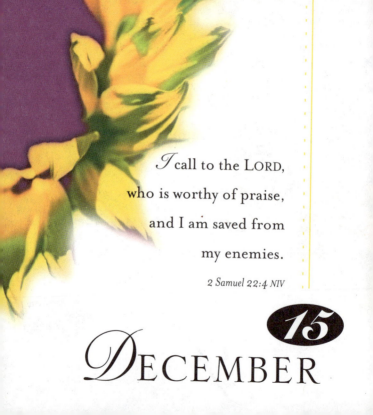

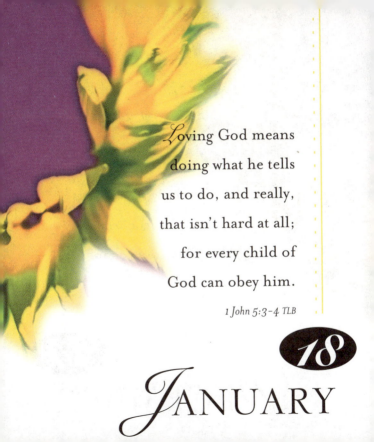

> *L*oving God means doing what he tells us to do, and really, that isn't hard at all; for every child of God can obey him.
>
> *1 John 5:3–4 TLB*

18 JANUARY

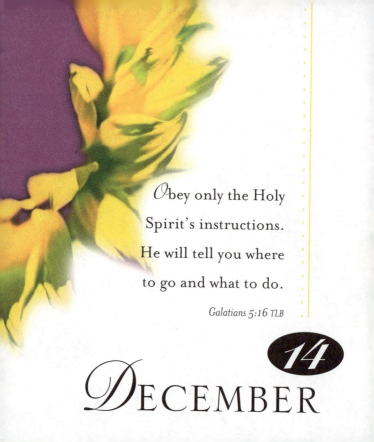

Obey only the Holy Spirit's instructions. He will tell you where to go and what to do.

Galatians 5:16 TLB

14
DECEMBER

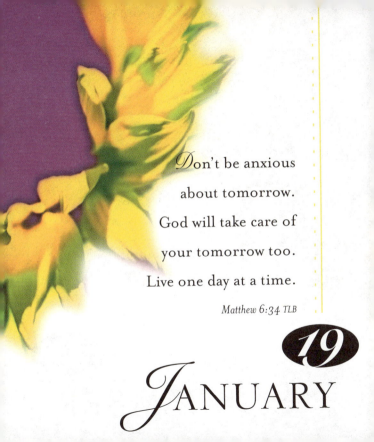

Don't be anxious about tomorrow. God will take care of your tomorrow too. Live one day at a time.

Matthew 6:34 TLB

19

JANUARY

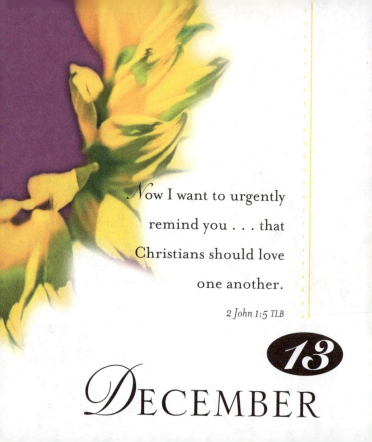

*N*ow I want to urgently remind you . . . that Christians should love one another.

2 John 1:5 TLB

*D*ECEMBER 13

He has showed you,
O man, what is good.
And what does the LORD
require of you? To act
justly and to love mercy
and to walk humbly
with your God.

Micah 6:8 NIV

20
JANUARY

> I know, my God, that you test men to see if they are good; for you enjoy good men.
>
> *1 Chronicles 29:17 TLB*

DECEMBER 12

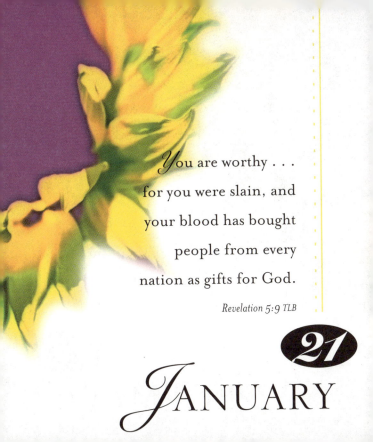

You are worthy . . .
for you were slain, and
your blood has bought
people from every
nation as gifts for God.

Revelation 5:9 TLB

21
JANUARY

You can have real love for everyone because your souls have been cleansed from selfishness and hatred when you trusted Christ.

1 Peter 1:22 TLB

11

DECEMBER

Patience develops strength of character in us and helps us trust God more each time we use it.

Romans 5:4 TLB

22
JANUARY

How good and pleasant it is when brothers live together in unity!

Psalm 133:1 NIV

10 DECEMBER

Let us stop just saying we love people; let us really love them, and show it by our actions.

1 John 3:18 TLB

23
JANUARY

For God so loved the world that he gave his one and only Son, that whoever believes in him shall not perish but have eternal life.

John 3:16 NIV

DECEMBER 9

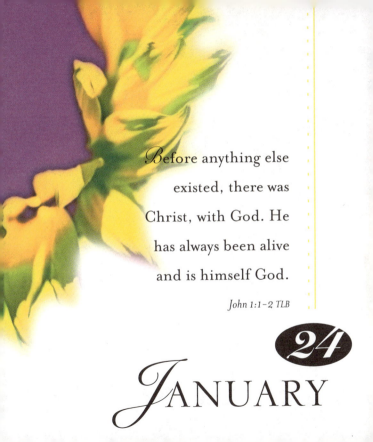

> *Before* anything else existed, there was Christ, with God. He has always been alive and is himself God.
>
> *John 1:1-2 TLB*

January 24

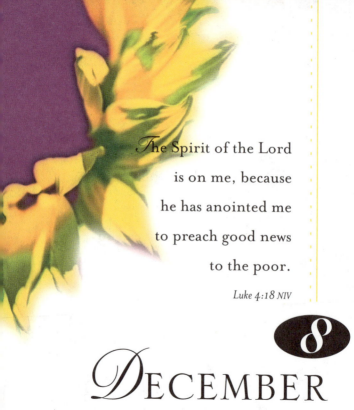

> The Spirit of the Lord is on me, because he has anointed me to preach good news to the poor.
>
> *Luke 4:18 NIV*

DECEMBER 8

The wise man saves for the future, but the foolish man spends whatever he gets.

Proverbs 21:20 TLB

25

JANUARY

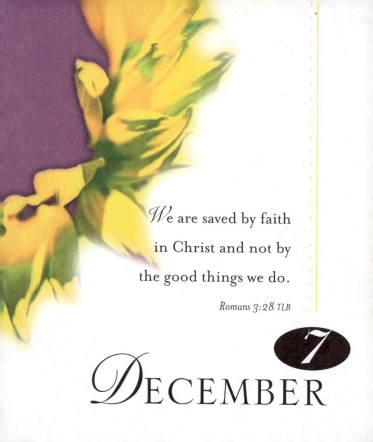

We are saved by faith in Christ and not by the good things we do.

Romans 3:28 TLB

December 7

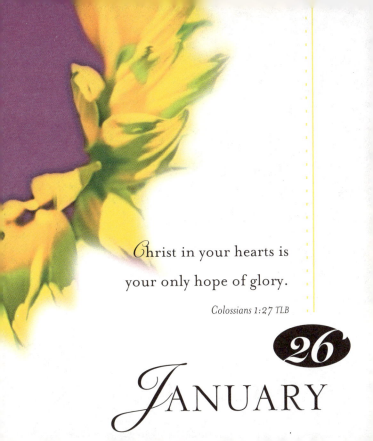

*C*hrist in your hearts is your only hope of glory.

Colossians 1:27 TLB

26

JANUARY

Be sure you know a person well before you vouch for his credit! Better refuse than suffer later.

Proverbs 11:15 TLB

DECEMBER 6

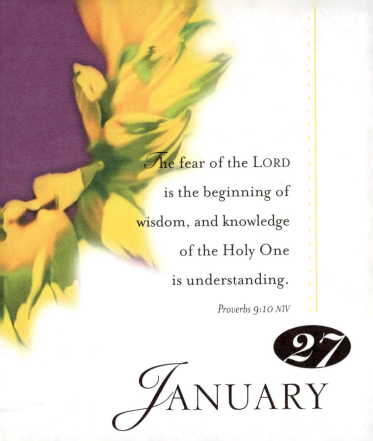

The fear of the LORD is the beginning of wisdom, and knowledge of the Holy One is understanding.

Proverbs 9:10 NIV

27 JANUARY

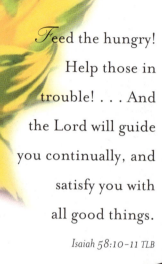

Feed the hungry! Help those in trouble! . . . And the Lord will guide you continually, and satisfy you with all good things.

Isaiah 58:10-11 TLB

5
DECEMBER

Now the dwelling of God is with men, and he will live with them. They will be his people, and God himself will be with them and be their God.

Revelation 21:3 NIV

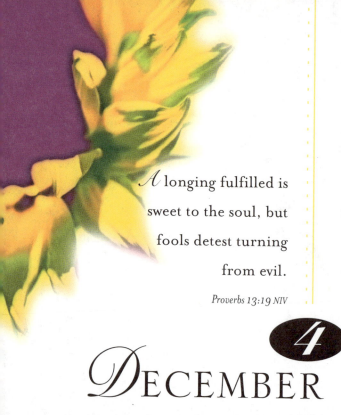

A longing fulfilled is sweet to the soul, but fools detest turning from evil.

Proverbs 13:19 NIV

DECEMBER 4

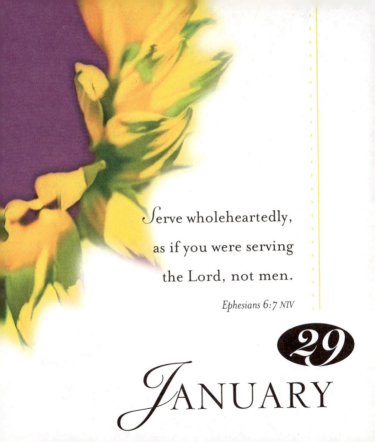

Serve wholeheartedly, as if you were serving the Lord, not men.

Ephesians 6:7 NIV

29 JANUARY

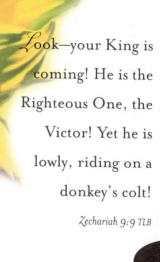

Look—your King is coming! He is the Righteous One, the Victor! Yet he is lowly, riding on a donkey's colt!

Zechariah 9:9 TLB

3
DECEMBER

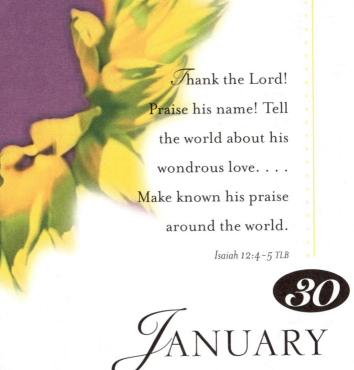

Thank the Lord! Praise his name! Tell the world about his wondrous love.... Make known his praise around the world.

Isaiah 12:4–5 TLB

30
JANUARY

I was a constant example to you in helping the poor; for I remembered the words of the Lord Jesus, "It is more blessed to give than to receive."

Acts 20:35 TLB

DECEMBER 2

Should we . . . complain when punished for our sins? Let us examine ourselves instead, and let us repent and turn again to the Lord.

Lamentations 3:39-40 TLB

31

JANUARY

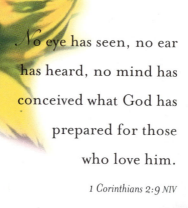

No eye has seen, no ear has heard, no mind has conceived what God has prepared for those who love him.

1 Corinthians 2:9 NIV

*D*ECEMBER *1*

Blessed are the pure in heart, for they will see God.

Matthew 5:8 NIV

FEBRUARY 1

> Has not the LORD made them one? In flesh and spirit they are his.... So guard yourself in your spirit, and do not break faith with the wife of your youth.
>
> *Malachi 2:15 NIV*

November 30

> Jehovah himself is caring for you! He is your defender. He protects you day and night.
>
> *Psalm 121:5-6 TLB*

FEBRUARY 2

Groundhog Day

You, O God, do see trouble and grief; you consider it to take it in hand. The victim commits himself to you; you are the helper of the fatherless.

Psalm 10:14 NIV

29 NOVEMBER

> The people walking in darkness have seen a great light; on those living in the land of the shadow of death a light has dawned.
>
> *Isaiah 9:2 NIV*

3 FEBRUARY

Listen, my dear brothers: Has not God chosen those who are poor in the eyes of the world to be rich in faith and to inherit the kingdom he promised those who love him?

James 2:5 NIV

28
NOVEMBER

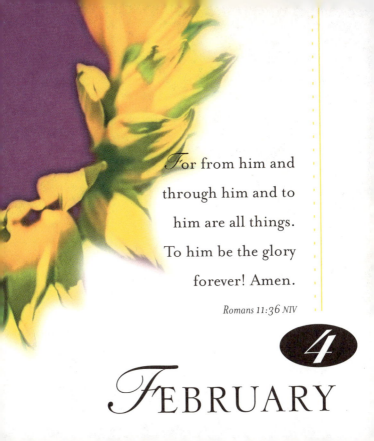

> For from him and through him and to him are all things. To him be the glory forever! Amen.
>
> *Romans 11:36 NIV*

FEBRUARY 4

But blessed is the man who trusts in the LORD, whose confidence is in him.

Jeremiah 17:7 NIV

27 NOVEMBER

Blessing, and glory, and wisdom, and thanksgiving, and honor, and power, and might, be to our God forever and forever.

Revelation 7:12 TLB

5 FEBRUARY

Let all rejoice who seek the Lord. Seek the Lord; yes, seek his strength and seek his face untiringly.

1 Chronicles 16:10–11 TLB

26
NOVEMBER

> Don't be fools; be wise: make the most of every opportunity you have for doing good.
>
> *Ephesians 5:15–16 TLB*

FEBRUARY 6

Anyone who says he is a Christian should live as Christ did.

1 John 2:6 TLB

25
NOVEMBER

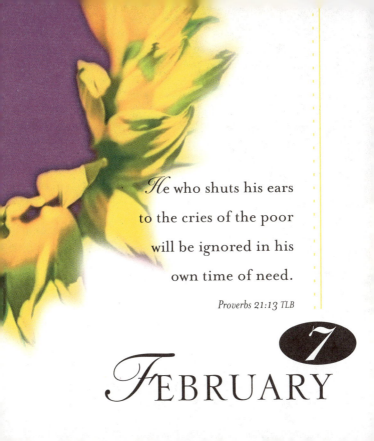

He who shuts his ears to the cries of the poor will be ignored in his own time of need.

Proverbs 21:13 TLB

FEBRUARY 7

The grass withers and the flowers fall, but the word of our God stands forever.

Isaiah 40:8 NIV

24

NOVEMBER

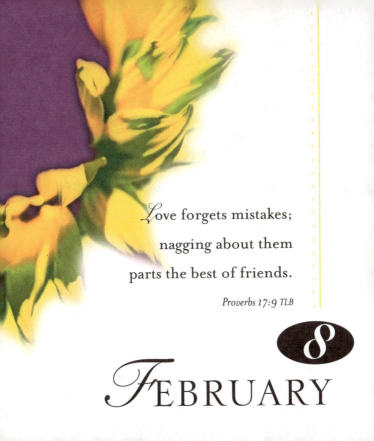

*Love forgets mistakes;
nagging about them
parts the best of friends.*

Proverbs 17:9 TLB

FEBRUARY 8

The heart of the discerning acquires knowledge; the ears of the wise seek it out.

Proverbs 18:15 NIV

23

NOVEMBER

O Bethlehem Ephrathah, you are but a small Judean village, yet you will be the birthplace of my King who is alive from everlasting ages past!

Micah 5:2 TLB

9
FEBRUARY

O Lord God! You have made the heavens and earth by your great power; nothing is too hard for you!

Jeremiah 32:17 TLB

22
November

Because God does not punish sinners instantly, people feel it is safe to do wrong. But . . . those who fear God will be better off.

Ecclesiastes 8:11–12 TLB

FEBRUARY 10

God is closely watching you, and he weighs carefully everything you do.

Proverbs 5:21 TLB

21

November

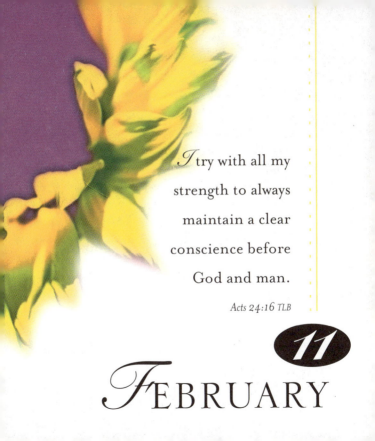

I try with all my strength to always maintain a clear conscience before God and man.

Acts 24:16 TLB

11
FEBRUARY

Dear friend, do not imitate what is evil but what is good. Anyone who does what is good is from God.

3 John 1:11 NIV

20
NOVEMBER

The Lord himself will choose the sign—a child shall be born to a virgin! And she shall call him Immanuel (meaning, "God is with us").

Isaiah 7:14 TLB

FEBRUARY 12

Lincoln's Birthday

The righteous man leads a blameless life; blessed are his children after him.

Proverbs 20:7 NIV

NOVEMBER 19

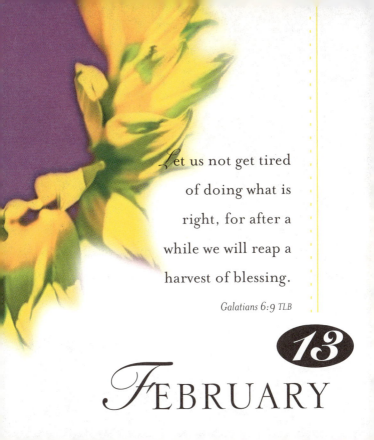

Let us not get tired of doing what is right, for after a while we will reap a harvest of blessing.

Galatians 6:9 TLB

13
FEBRUARY

As the Spirit of the Lord works within us, we become more and more like him.

2 Corinthians 3:18 TLB

18 NOVEMBER

Give thanks to the LORD, for he is good; his love endures forever.

1 Chronicles 16:34 NIV

14

FEBRUARY

Valentine's Day

Above all, love each other deeply, because love covers over a multitude of sins.

1 Peter 4:8 NIV

17

NOVEMBER

Peacemakers who sow in peace raise a harvest of righteousness.

James 3:18 NIV

15
FEBRUARY

Children are a gift from God; they are his reward.

Psalm 127:3 TLB

NOVEMBER 16

Though you have scorned my laws from earliest time, yet you may still return to me. . . . Come and I will forgive you.

Malachi 3:7 TLB

16

FEBRUARY

> *Yet the* LORD *longs to be gracious to you; he rises to show you compassion. For the* LORD *is a God of justice. Blessed are all who wait for him!*
>
> *Isaiah 30:18 NIV*

NOVEMBER 15

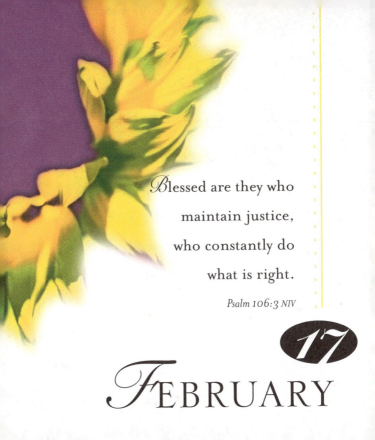

Blessed are they who maintain justice, who constantly do what is right.

Psalm 106:3 NIV

17

FEBRUARY

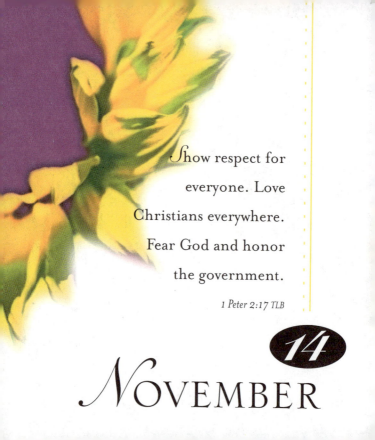

> Show respect for everyone. Love Christians everywhere. Fear God and honor the government.
>
> *1 Peter 2:17 TLB*

14
November

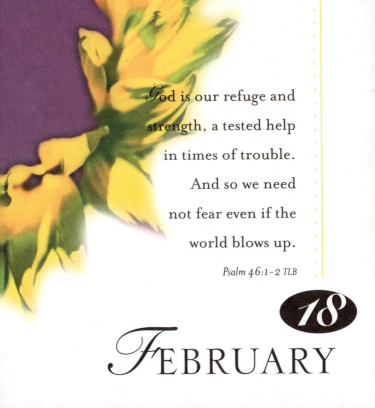

God is our refuge and strength, a tested help in times of trouble. And so we need not fear even if the world blows up.

Psalm 46:1-2 TLB

18
FEBRUARY

> Because the Sovereign LORD helps me, I will not be disgraced. Therefore have I set my face like flint, and I know I will not be put to shame.
>
> *Isaiah 50:7 NIV*

NOVEMBER 13

Yet, O Lord, you are our Father. We are the clay, you are the potter; we are all the work of your hand.

Isaiah 64:8 NIV

FEBRUARY 19

Physical training is of some value, but godliness has value for all things, holding promise for both the present life and the life to come.

1 Timothy 4:8 NIV

November 12

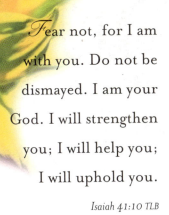

*F*ear not, for I am with you. Do not be dismayed. I am your God. I will strengthen you; I will help you; I will uphold you.

Isaiah 41:10 TLB

20

FEBRUARY

Rejoice in the Lord always: and again I say, Rejoice.

Philippians 4:4 KJV

November

11

Veterans Day

I have not come to call the righteous, but sinners to repentance.

Luke 5:32 NIV

21
FEBRUARY

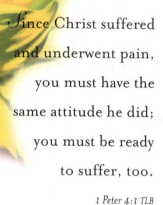

Since Christ suffered and underwent pain, you must have the same attitude he did; you must be ready to suffer, too.

1 Peter 4:1 TLB

10
NOVEMBER

Praise be to his glorious name forever; may the whole earth be filled with his glory. Amen and Amen.

Psalm 72:19 NIV

22 FEBRUARY

Washington's Birthday

A man should leave his father and mother, and be forever united to his wife. The two shall become one.

Matthew 19:5-6 TLB

NOVEMBER 9

One's nationality or race or education or social position is unimportant.... Whether a person has Christ is what matters.

Colossians 3:11 TLB

23
FEBRUARY

God makes us ready for heaven—makes us right in God's sight—when we put our faith and trust in Christ to save us.

Romans 1:17 TLB

November 8

For the kingdom of God is not a matter of eating and drinking, but of righteousness, peace and joy in the Holy Spirit.

Romans 14:17 NIV

24
FEBRUARY

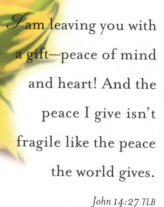

I am leaving you with a gift—peace of mind and heart! And the peace I give isn't fragile like the peace the world gives.

John 14:27 TLB

NOVEMBER 7

*W*hen I am afraid,

I will trust in you.

Psalm 56:3 NIV

25

FEBRUARY

The eyes of all look to you, and you give them their food at the proper time.

Psalm 145:15 NIV

NOVEMBER 6

> Get to know the God of your fathers. Worship and serve him with a clean heart and a willing mind.
>
> *1 Chronicles 28:9 TLB*

FEBRUARY 26

You are the salt of the earth. But if the salt loses its saltiness, how can it be made salty again? It is no longer good for anything.

Matthew 5:13 NIV

5

NOVEMBER

Create in me a new, clean heart, O God, filled with clean thoughts and right desires.

Psalm 51:10 TLB

27 FEBRUARY

"I know the plans I have for you," declares the LORD, "plans to prosper you and not to harm you, plans to give you hope and a future."

Jeremiah 29:11 NIV

November

4

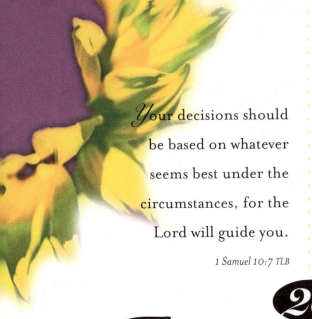

Your decisions should be based on whatever seems best under the circumstances, for the Lord will guide you.

1 Samuel 10:7 TLB

28
FEBRUARY

*Y*our attitudes and thoughts must all be constantly changing for the better.

Ephesians 4:23 TLB

3
NOVEMBER

> *D*ay by day the Lord
> also pours out his
> steadfast love upon me,
> and through the night
> I sing his songs
> and pray to God who
> gives me life.
>
> *Psalm 42:8 TLB*

29
FEBRUARY

Stay away from any Christian who spends his days in laziness and does not follow the ideal of hard work.

2 Thessalonians 3:6 TLB

November 2

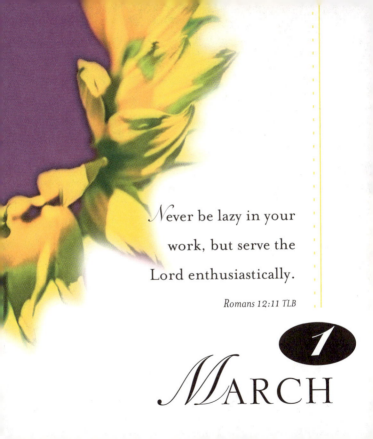

*N*ever be lazy in your work, but serve the Lord enthusiastically.

Romans 12:11 TLB

*M*ARCH 1

The man who finds a wife finds a good thing; she is a blessing to him from the Lord.

Proverbs 18:22 TLB

1

NOVEMBER

Don't store up treasures here on earth where they can erode away or may be stolen. Store them in heaven.

Matthew 6:19-20 TLB

MARCH 2

Happy is the generous man, the one who feeds the poor.

Proverbs 22:9 TLB

31
OCTOBER
Reformation Day

> Christ himself is the Creator who made everything in heaven and earth, the things we can see and the things we can't.
>
> *Colossians 1:16 TLB*

I have called you by name; you are mine. When you go through deep waters and great trouble, I will be with you.

Isaiah 43:1-2 TLB

30
OCTOBER

> *Listen: Jehovah is our God, Jehovah alone. You must love him with all your heart, soul, and might.*
>
> Deuteronomy 6:4–5 TLB

MARCH 4

This should be your ambition: to live a quiet life, minding your own business and doing your own work.

1 Thessalonians 4:11 TLB

29
OCTOBER

> God's laws are perfect.
> They protect us, make
> us wise, and give us
> joy and light.
>
> *Psalm 19:7-8 TLB*

March 5

In your hearts set apart Christ as Lord. Always be prepared to give an answer to everyone who asks you to give the reason for the hope that you have.

1 Peter 3:15 NIV

28

OCTOBER

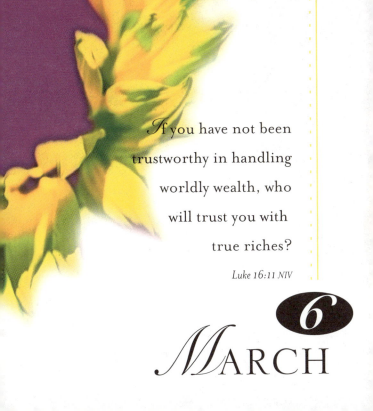

If you have not been trustworthy in handling worldly wealth, who will trust you with true riches?

Luke 16:11 NIV

MARCH 6

I know it is not within the power of man to map his life and plan his course—so you correct me, Lord; but please be gentle.

Jeremiah 10:23-24 TLB

27

OCTOBER

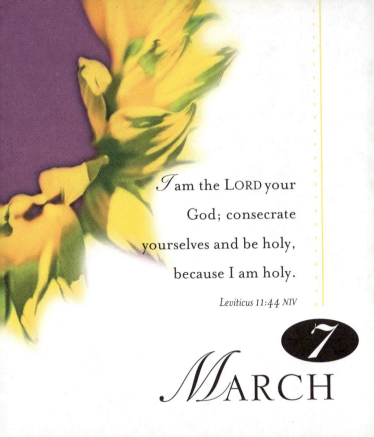

> I am the LORD your God; consecrate yourselves and be holy, because I am holy.
>
> *Leviticus 11:44 NIV*

MARCH 7

If you suffer as a Christian, do not be ashamed, but praise God that you bear that name.

1 Peter 4:16 NIV

26

OCTOBER

*W*hat I want from you is your true thanks; I want your promises fulfilled. I want you to trust me.

Psalm 50:14–15 TLB

8

MARCH

Above all else, guard your affections. For they influence everything else in your life.

Proverbs 4:23 TLB

OCTOBER 25

Be ye stedfast, unmovable, always abounding in the work of the Lord, forasmuch as ye know that your labour is not in vain in the Lord.

1 Corinthians 15:58 KJV

9
MARCH

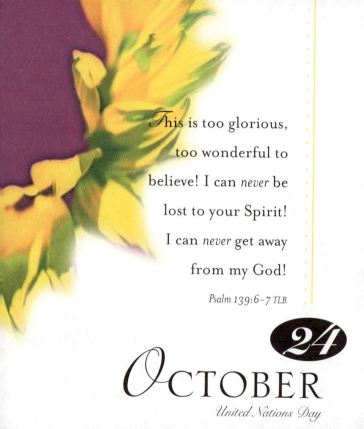

This is too glorious, too wonderful to believe! I can *never* be lost to your Spirit! I can *never* get away from my God!

Psalm 139:6–7 TLB

October 24

United Nations Day

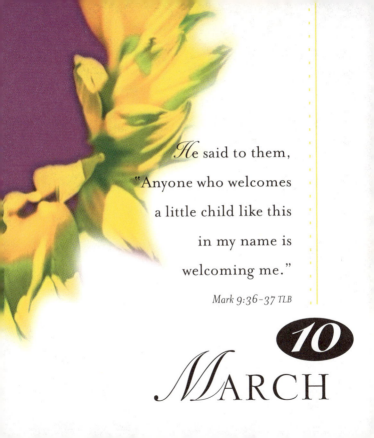

*H*e said to them, "Anyone who welcomes a little child like this in my name is welcoming me."

Mark 9:36-37 TLB

10 MARCH

Do not conform any longer to the pattern of this world, but be transformed by the renewing of your mind. Then you will be able to test and approve what God's will is.

Romans 12:2 NIV

23
October

> *We can make our plans, but the final outcome is in God's hands.*
>
> Proverbs 16:1 TLB

MARCH 11

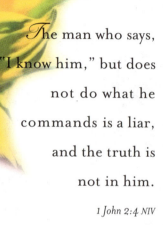

The man who says, "I know him," but does not do what he commands is a liar, and the truth is not in him.

1 John 2:4 NIV

OCTOBER 22

> I will give you a new heart and put a new spirit in you; I will remove from you your heart of stone and give you a heart of flesh.
>
> *Ezekiel 36:26 NIV*

MARCH 12

My brothers, as believers in our glorious Lord Jesus Christ, don't show favoritism.

James 2:1 NIV

OCTOBER 21

Don't quarrel with anyone. Be at peace with everyone, just as much as possible.

Romans 12:18 TLB

13
MARCH

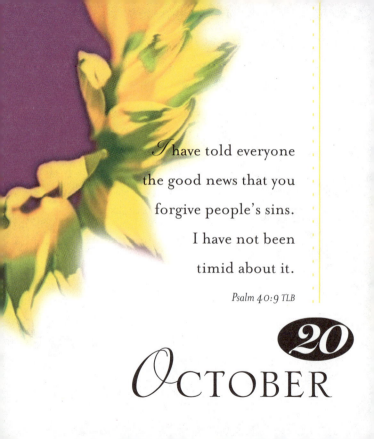

I have told everyone the good news that you forgive people's sins. I have not been timid about it.

Psalm 40:9 TLB

OCTOBER 20

People who want to get rich fall into temptation and a trap and into many foolish and harmful desires that plunge men into ruin and destruction.

1 Timothy 6:9 NIV

14
MARCH

*Y*es, be bold and strong! Banish fear and doubt! For remember, the Lord your God is with you wherever you go.

Joshua 1:9 TLB

19 OCTOBER

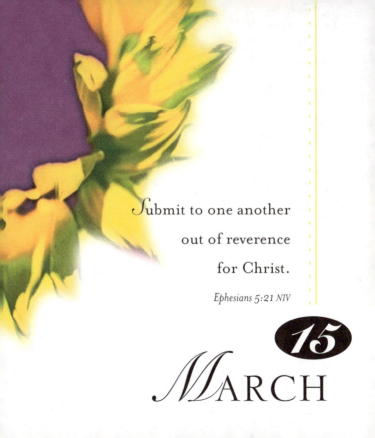

Submit to one another out of reverence for Christ.

Ephesians 5:21 NIV

15

MARCH

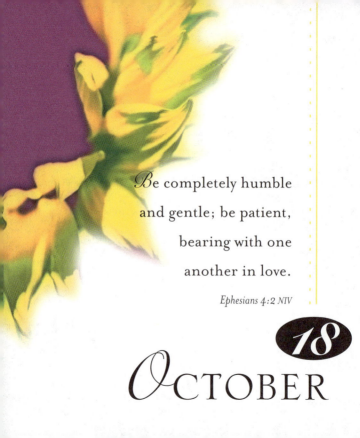

Be completely humble and gentle; be patient, bearing with one another in love.

Ephesians 4:2 NIV

18

OCTOBER

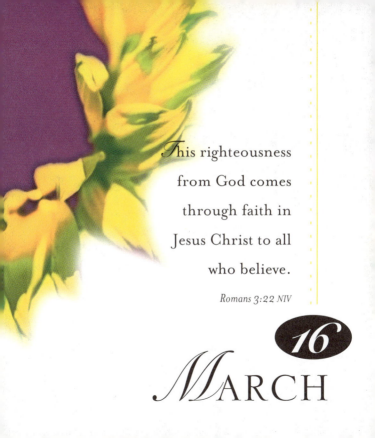

> This righteousness from God comes through faith in Jesus Christ to all who believe.
>
> *Romans 3:22 NIV*

MARCH 16

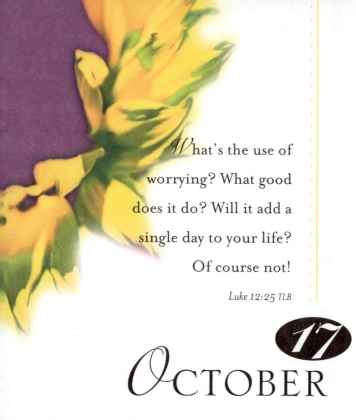

*W*hat's the use of worrying? What good does it do? Will it add a single day to your life? Of course not!

Luke 12:25 TLB

OCTOBER 17

To do what is right and just is more acceptable to the LORD than sacrifice.

Proverbs 21:3 NIV

17 MARCH

St. Patrick's Day

Don't worry about anything; instead, pray about everything; tell God your needs, and don't forget to thank him for his answers.

Philippians 4:6 TLB

OCTOBER 16

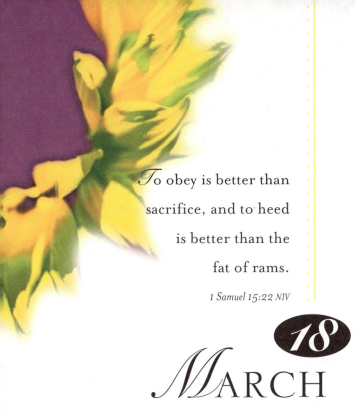

To obey is better than sacrifice, and to heed is better than the fat of rams.

1 Samuel 15:22 NIV

18 MARCH

*O*nly in returning to me and waiting for me will you be saved; in quietness and confidence is your strength.

Isaiah 30:15 TLB

15
OCTOBER

*O*bey your father and your mother. Take to heart all of their advice; keep in mind everything they tell you.

Proverbs 6:20-21 TLB

19
*M*ARCH

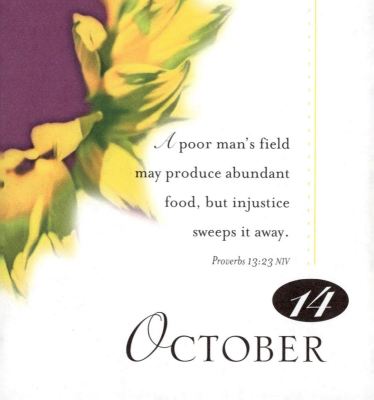

A poor man's field may produce abundant food, but injustice sweeps it away.

Proverbs 13:23 NIV

14
October

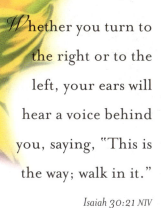

*W*hether you turn to the right or to the left, your ears will hear a voice behind you, saying, "This is the way; walk in it."

Isaiah 30:21 NIV

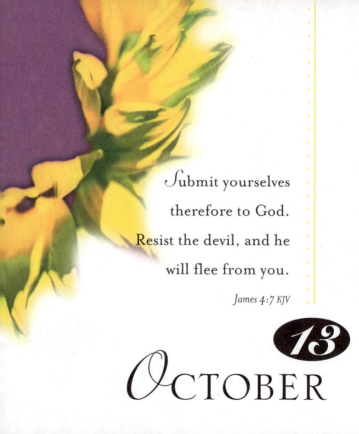

Submit yourselves therefore to God. Resist the devil, and he will flee from you.

James 4:7 KJV

13

OCTOBER

Tell the truth. Be fair. Live at peace with everyone. Don't plot harm to others.

Zechariah 8:16–17 TLB

MARCH 21

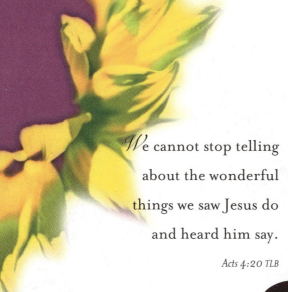

We cannot stop telling about the wonderful things we saw Jesus do and heard him say.

Acts 4:20 TLB

OCTOBER **12**

Columbus Day

*O*nly the Lord knows! He searches all hearts and examines deepest motives so he can give to each person his right reward.

Jeremiah 17:10 TLB

MARCH 22

> *No* one can say, "Jesus is Lord," and really mean it, unless the Holy Spirit is helping him.
>
> *1 Corinthians 12:3 TLB*

October 11

> Renounce your sins by doing what is right, and your wickedness by being kind to the oppressed. It may be that then your prosperity will continue.
>
> *Daniel 4:27 NIV*

MARCH 23

The Lord is good.
When trouble comes,
he is the place to go!
And he knows everyone
who trusts in him!

Nahum 1:7 TLB

10
OCTOBER

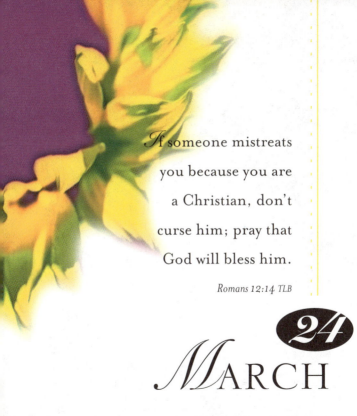

> *If* someone mistreats you because you are a Christian, don't curse him; pray that God will bless him.
>
> *Romans 12:14 TLB*

MARCH 24

> Not by might, nor by power, but by my spirit, saith the LORD of hosts.
>
> *Zechariah 4:6 KJV*

OCTOBER 9

I will reject all selfishness and stay away from every evil. I will not tolerate anyone who secretly slanders his neighbors.

Psalm 101:4–5 TLB

25

MARCH

He changes times and seasons.... He gives wisdom to the wise and knowledge to the discerning.

Daniel 2:21 NIV

October 8

Love your enemies! Pray for those who persecute you! In that way you will be acting as true sons of your Father in heaven.

Matthew 5:44–45 TLB

26

MARCH

If we confess our sins, he is faithful and just to forgive us our sins, and to cleanse us from all unrighteousness.

1 John 1:9 KJV

7

OCTOBER

> The end of a matter is better than its beginning, and patience is better than pride.
>
> *Ecclesiastes 7:8 NIV*

March 27

Do not think of yourself more highly than you ought, but rather think of yourself with sober judgment, in accordance with the measure of faith God has given you.

Romans 12:3 NIV

6

OCTOBER

> *I consider my life worth nothing to me, if only I may finish the race and complete the task the Lord Jesus has given me—the task of testifying to the gospel of God's grace.*
>
> Acts 20:24 NIV

28 MARCH

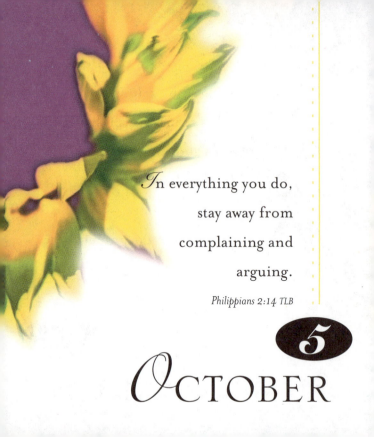

*In everything you do,
stay away from
complaining and
arguing.*

Philippians 2:14 TLB

OCTOBER 5

A man who refuses to admit his mistakes can never be successful. But if he confesses and forsakes them, he gets another chance.

Proverbs 28:13 TLB

29 MARCH

Blessed be the name of God for ever and ever: for wisdom and might are his.

Daniel 2:20 KJV

OCTOBER 4

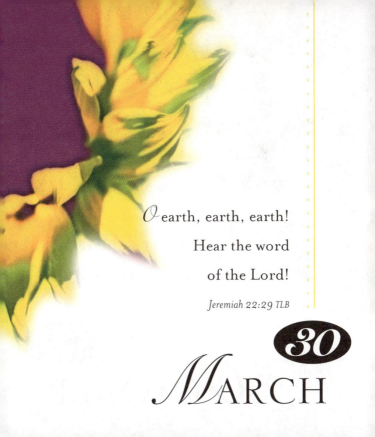

O earth, earth, earth!
Hear the word
of the Lord!

Jeremiah 22:29 TLB

30

MARCH

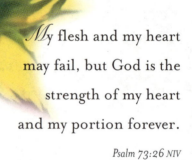

My flesh and my heart may fail, but God is the strength of my heart and my portion forever.

Psalm 73:26 NIV

OCTOBER 3

The Lord sees every heart and understands and knows every thought. If you seek him, you will find him.

1 Chronicles 28:9 TLB

31

MARCH

> Some trust in chariots, and some in horses: but we will remember the name of the LORD our God.
>
> *Psalm 20:7 KJV*

OCTOBER 2

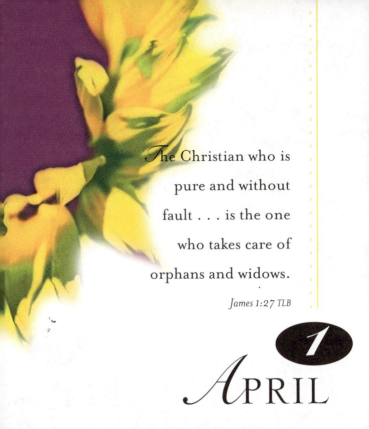

The Christian who is pure and without fault . . . is the one who takes care of orphans and widows.

James 1:27 TLB

April 1

Holy, holy, holy is the Lord God Almighty, who was, and is, and is to come.

Revelation 4:8 NIV

OCTOBER 1

He was taken out of the city, carrying his cross to the place known as "The Skull." . . . There they crucified him.

John 19:17–18 TLB

April 2

*C*heerfully share your home with those who need a meal or a place to stay for the night.

1 Peter 4:9 TLB

30

SEPTEMBER

*W*hy are you looking in a tomb for someone who is alive? He isn't here! He has come back to life again!

Luke 24:5-6 TLB

3

APRIL

The greatest among you will be your servant.

Matthew 23:11 NIV

29

SEPTEMBER

I will instruct you and teach you in the way you should go; I will counsel you and watch over you.

Psalm 32:8 NIV

4

APRIL

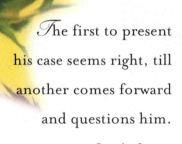

The first to present his case seems right, till another comes forward and questions him.

Proverbs 18:17 NIV

28

SEPTEMBER

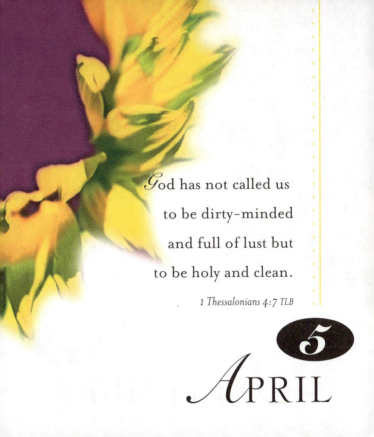

God has not called us to be dirty-minded and full of lust but to be holy and clean.

1 Thessalonians 4:7 TLB

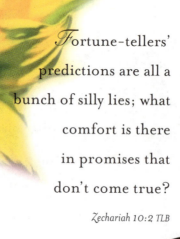

Fortune-tellers' predictions are all a bunch of silly lies; what comfort is there in promises that don't come true?

Zechariah 10:2 TLB

SEPTEMBER 27

He was pierced for our transgressions, he was crushed for our iniquities; the punishment that brought us peace was upon him, and by his wounds we are healed.

Isaiah 53:5 NIV

Praise be to the Lord,

to God our Savior, who

daily bears our burdens.

Psalm 68:19 NIV

26

SEPTEMBER

Watch out! Be on your guard against all kinds of greed; a man's life does not consist in the abundance of his possessions.

Luke 12:15 NIV

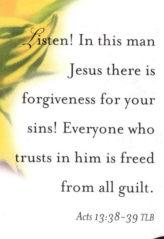

Listen! In this man Jesus there is forgiveness for your sins! Everyone who trusts in him is freed from all guilt.

Acts 13:38-39 TLB

25
SEPTEMBER

We know that since Christ was raised from the dead, he cannot die again; death no longer has mastery over him.

Romans 6:9 NIV

April 8

"*If* you are willing, you can make me clean." Filled with compassion, Jesus reached out his hand and touched the man. "I am willing," he said. "Be clean!"

Mark 1:40-41 NIV

24

SEPTEMBER

> Confess your sins to each other and pray for each other so that you may be healed. The prayer of a righteous man is powerful and effective.
>
> *James 5:16 NIV*

April 9

> How beautiful on the mountains are the feet of those who bring good news, who proclaim peace . . . who proclaim salvation, who say to Zion, "Your God reigns!"
>
> *Isaiah 52:7 NIV*

23
SEPTEMBER

O righteous God, who searches minds and hearts, bring to an end the violence of the wicked and make the righteous secure.

Psalm 7:9 NIV

10
APRIL

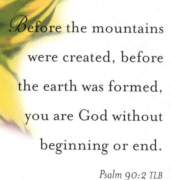

*B*efore the mountains were created, before the earth was formed, you are God without beginning or end.

Psalm 90:2 TLB

22
SEPTEMBER

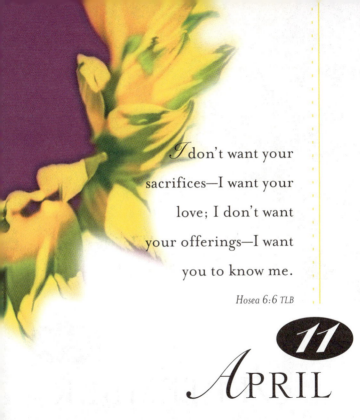

I don't want your sacrifices—I want your love; I don't want your offerings—I want you to know me.

Hosea 6:6 TLB

11

APRIL

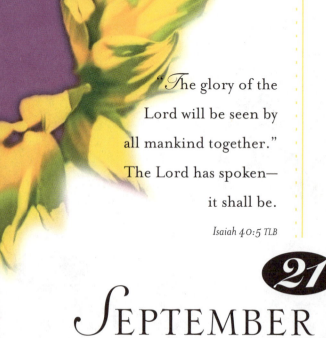

"The glory of the Lord will be seen by all mankind together." The Lord has spoken—it shall be.

Isaiah 40:5 TLB

21 SEPTEMBER

Repent ye therefore, and be converted, that your sins may be blotted out, when the times of refreshing shall come from the presence of the Lord.

Acts 3:19 KJV

Rejoice with those who rejoice; mourn with those who mourn.

Romans 12:15 NIV

20 SEPTEMBER

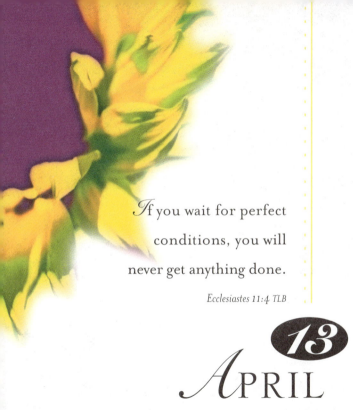

If you wait for perfect conditions, you will never get anything done.

Ecclesiastes 11:4 TLB

13
APRIL

And this is his command: to believe in the name of his Son, Jesus Christ, and to love one another as he commanded us.

1 John 3:23 NIV

19

SEPTEMBER

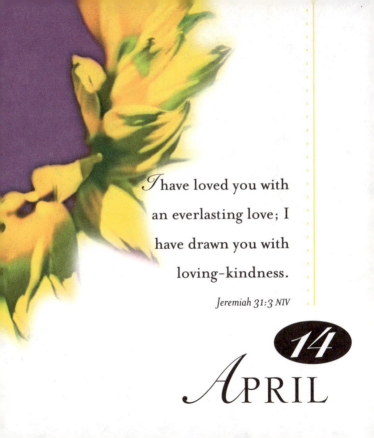

I have loved you with an everlasting love; I have drawn you with loving-kindness.

Jeremiah 31:3 NIV

14

*A*PRIL

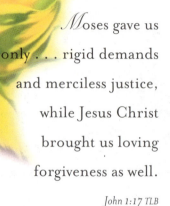

Moses gave us only . . . rigid demands and merciless justice, while Jesus Christ brought us loving forgiveness as well.

John 1:17 TLB

18
SEPTEMBER

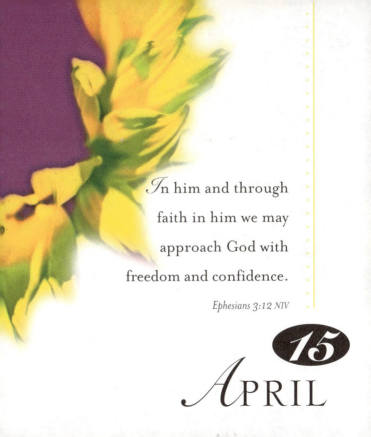

In him and through faith in him we may approach God with freedom and confidence.

Ephesians 3:12 NIV

15 APRIL

I will bless the Lord and not forget the glorious things he does for me.

Psalm 103:2 TLB

17

SEPTEMBER

Citizenship Day

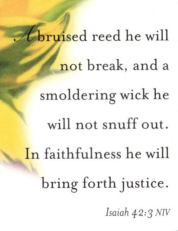

> A bruised reed he will not break, and a smoldering wick he will not snuff out. In faithfulness he will bring forth justice.
>
> *Isaiah 42:3 NIV*

16 APRIL

You must return to your God; maintain love and justice, and wait for your God always.

Hosea 12:6 NIV

16

SEPTEMBER

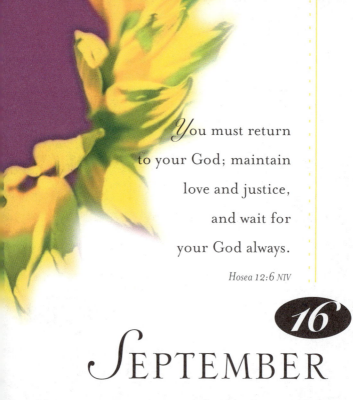

*A*way with your hymns of praise. . . . I want to see a mighty flood of justice—a torrent of doing good.

Amos 5:23–24 TLB

17
*A*PRIL

Stop lying to each other; tell the truth, for we are parts of each other and when we lie to each other we are hurting ourselves.

Ephesians 4:25 TLB

15

SEPTEMBER

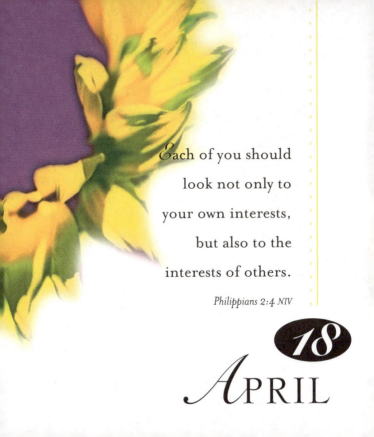

Each of you should look not only to your own interests, but also to the interests of others.

Philippians 2:4 NIV

18
APRIL

*W*here there are no oxen, the manger is empty, but from the strength of an ox comes an abundant harvest.

Proverbs 14:4 NIV

14

SEPTEMBER

No temptation is irresistible. You can trust God to keep the temptation from becoming so strong that you can't stand up against it.

1 Corinthians 10:13 TLB

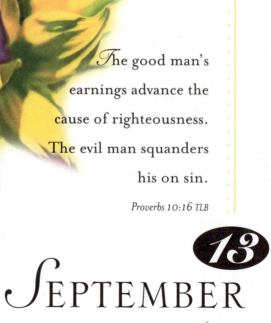

The good man's earnings advance the cause of righteousness. The evil man squanders his on sin.

Proverbs 10:16 TLB

13
SEPTEMBER

A wicked messenger falls into trouble, but a trustworthy envoy brings healing.

Proverbs 13:17 NIV

20 APRIL

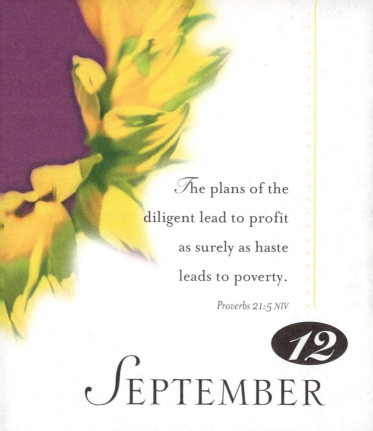

The plans of the diligent lead to profit as surely as haste leads to poverty.

Proverbs 21:5 NIV

12

SEPTEMBER

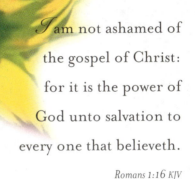

I am not ashamed of the gospel of Christ: for it is the power of God unto salvation to every one that believeth.

Romans 1:16 KJV

21

*A*PRIL

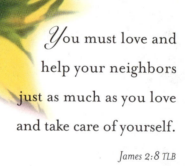

You must love and help your neighbors just as much as you love and take care of yourself.

James 2:8 TLB

11

SEPTEMBER

> *God released him from the horrors of death and brought him back to life again, for death could not keep this man within its grip.*
>
> Acts 2:24 TLB

22 APRIL

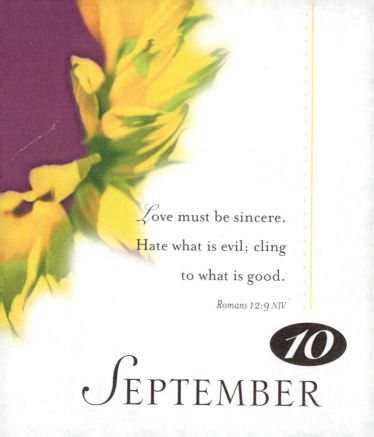

*L*ove must be sincere.
Hate what is evil; cling
to what is good.

Romans 12:9 NIV

10
SEPTEMBER

And this gospel of the kingdom will be preached in the whole world as a testimony to all nations, and then the end will come.

Matthew 24:14 NIV

23
APRIL

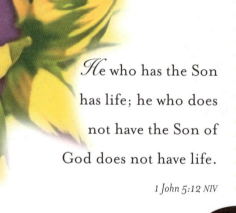

He who has the Son has life; he who does not have the Son of God does not have life.

1 John 5:12 NIV

SEPTEMBER 9

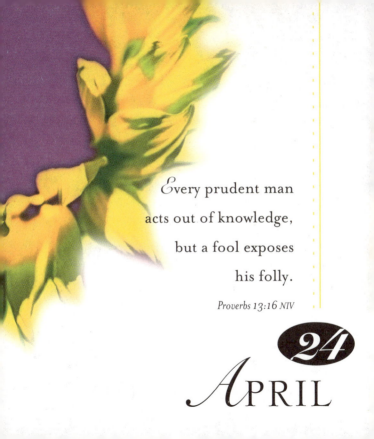

*E*very prudent man acts out of knowledge, but a fool exposes his folly.

Proverbs 13:16 NIV

24 APRIL

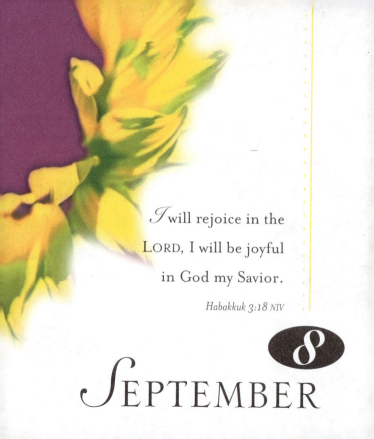

I will rejoice in the LORD, I will be joyful in God my Savior.

Habakkuk 3:18 NIV

SEPTEMBER 8

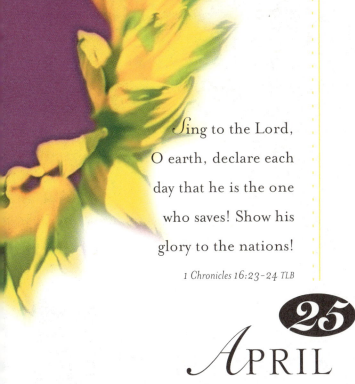

Sing to the Lord, O earth, declare each day that he is the one who saves! Show his glory to the nations!

1 Chronicles 16:23-24 TLB

25 APRIL

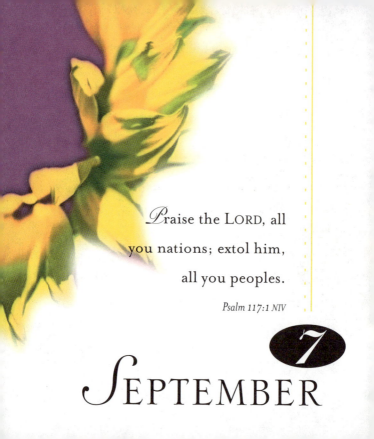

> Praise the LORD, all you nations; extol him, all you peoples.
>
> *Psalm 117:1 NIV*

SEPTEMBER 7

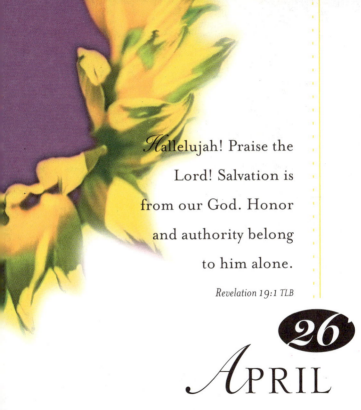

Hallelujah! Praise the Lord! Salvation is from our God. Honor and authority belong to him alone.

Revelation 19:1 TLB

26 APRIL

I want you to share your food with the hungry and bring right into your own homes those who are helpless.

Isaiah 58:7 TLB

SEPTEMBER 6

I plead with you to give your bodies to God. Let them be a living sacrifice, holy—the kind he can accept.

Romans 12:1 TLB

27 APRIL

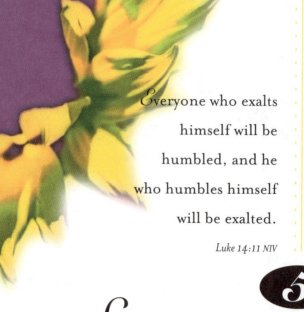

Everyone who exalts himself will be humbled, and he who humbles himself will be exalted.

Luke 14:11 NIV

5
SEPTEMBER

Be beautiful inside, in your hearts, with the lasting charm of a gentle and quiet spirit that is so precious to God.

1 Peter 3:4 TLB

28 APRIL

Be truly glad! There is wonderful joy ahead, even though the going is rough for a while down here.

1 Peter 1:6 TLB

SEPTEMBER 4

A wise man's words express deep streams of thought.

Proverbs 18:4 TLB

29 APRIL

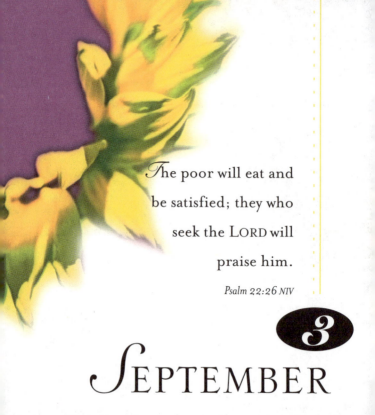

> The poor will eat and be satisfied; they who seek the LORD will praise him.
>
> *Psalm 22:26 NIV*

SEPTEMBER 3

*O*h, that their hearts would be inclined to fear me and keep all my commands always, so that it might go well with them and their children forever!

Deuteronomy 5:29 NIV

*N*ever envy the wicked! . . . Trust in the Lord instead. Be kind and good to others; then you will live safely.

Psalm 37:1, 3 TLB

SEPTEMBER 2

Arise, O God, judge the earth: for thou shalt inherit all nations.

Psalm 82:8 KJV

MAY 1

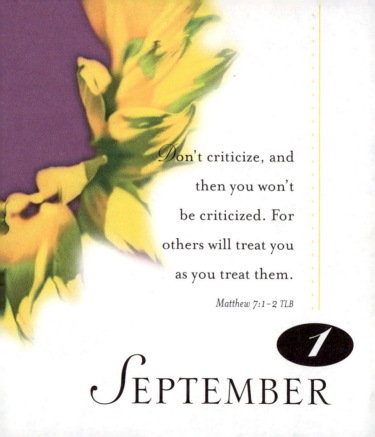

> Don't criticize, and then you won't be criticized. For others will treat you as you treat them.
>
> *Matthew 7:1–2 TLB*

SEPTEMBER 1

> *It is better to heed a wise man's rebuke than to listen to the song of fools.*
>
> Ecclesiastes 7:5 NIV

MAY 2

*P*ut on the full armor of God, so that when the day of evil comes, you may be able to stand your ground, and after you have done everything, to stand.

Ephesians 6:13 NIV

31

AUGUST

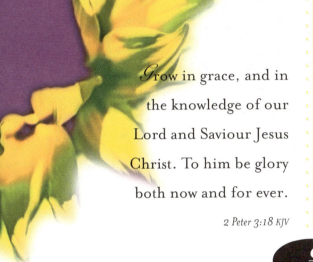

Grow in grace, and in the knowledge of our Lord and Saviour Jesus Christ. To him be glory both now and for ever.

2 Peter 3:18 KJV

3 MAY

Anyone, then, who knows the good he ought to do and doesn't do it, sins.

James 4:17 NIV

30
AUGUST

We never give up. Though our bodies are dying, our inner strength in the Lord is growing every day.

2 Corinthians 4:16 TLB

4 May

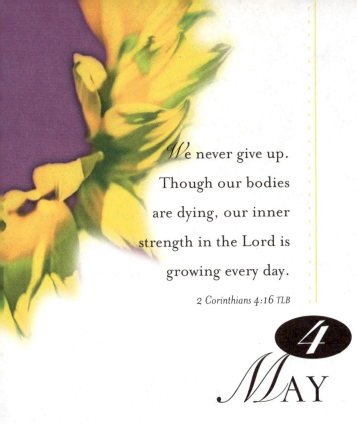

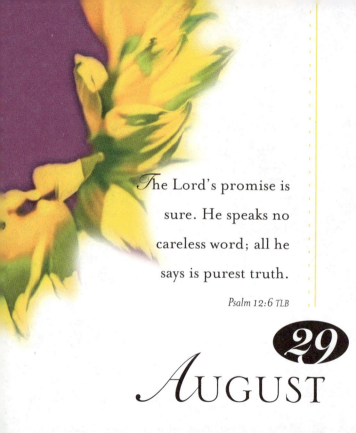

The Lord's promise is sure. He speaks no careless word; all he says is purest truth.

Psalm 12:6 TLB

29
AUGUST

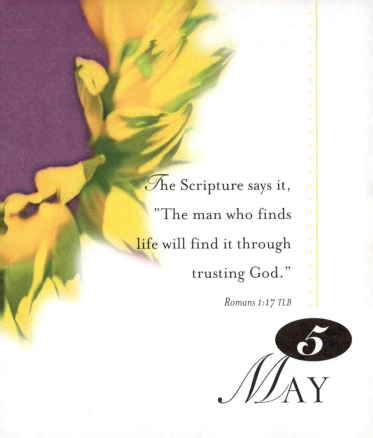

The Scripture says it, "The man who finds life will find it through trusting God."

Romans 1:17 TLB

MAY 5

As for God, his way is perfect; the word of the Lord is true. He shields all who hide behind him.

2 Samuel 22:31 TLB

28
August

Lift your eyes to see what God is doing all around the world; then you will say, "Truly, the Lord's great power goes far beyond our borders!"

Malachi 1:5 TLB

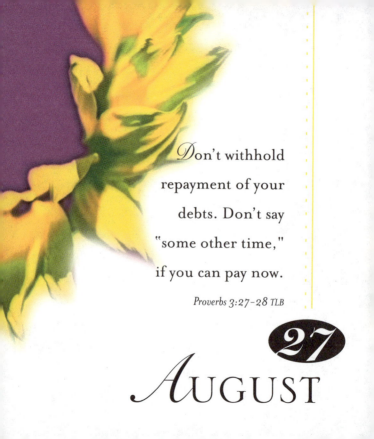

Don't withhold repayment of your debts. Don't say "some other time," if you can pay now.

Proverbs 3:27–28 TLB

27

AUGUST

*D*elight yourself in the LORD and he will give you the desires of your heart.

Psalm 37:4 NIV

MAY 7

We who believe are carefully joined together with Christ as parts of a beautiful, constantly growing temple for God.

Ephesians 2:21 TLB

26 AUGUST

Be careful not to do your "acts of righteousness" before men, to be seen by them. If you do, you will have no reward from your Father in heaven.

Matthew 6:1 NIV

Don't be weary in prayer; keep at it; watch for God's answers, and remember to be thankful when they come.

Colossians 4:2 TLB

25

AUGUST

$\mathcal{G}$reat is his faithfulness; his loving-kindness begins afresh each day. My soul claims the Lord as my inheritance.

Lamentations 3:23-24 TLB

Blessed are those who hunger and thirst for righteousness, for they will be filled.

Matthew 5:6 NIV

24
AUGUST

Whatsoever things are true . . . honest . . . just . . . pure . . . lovely . . . of good report; if there be any virtue, and if there be any praise, think on these things.

Philippians 4:8 KJV

He bestows rain on the earth; he sends water upon the countryside. The lowly he sets on high, and those who mourn are lifted to safety.

Job 5:10–11 NIV

23
AUGUST

The LORD confides in those who fear him; he makes his covenant known to them.

Psalm 25:14 NIV

MAY 11

Lead me, O Lord, in your righteousness . . . make straight your way before me.

Psalm 5:8 NIV

22 AUGUST

Seek the LORD while he may be found; call on him while he is near.

Isaiah 55:6 NIV

MAY 12

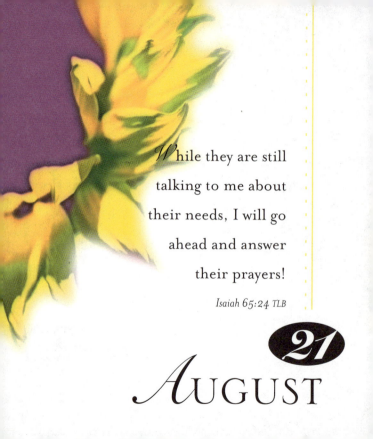

> While they are still talking to me about their needs, I will go ahead and answer their prayers!
>
> *Isaiah 65:24 TLB*

August 21

Keep a close watch on all you do and think. Stay true to what is right and God will bless you and use you to help others.

1 Timothy 4:16 TLB

MAY 13

> Anyone who says he is a Christian but doesn't control his sharp tongue is just fooling himself, and his religion isn't worth much.
>
> *James 1:26 TLB*

August 20

Do not let any unwholesome talk come out of your mouths, but only what is helpful for building others up according to their needs.

Ephesians 4:29 NIV

Happy are those who are strong in the Lord, who want above all else to follow your steps.

Psalm 84:5 TLB

19
AUGUST

$\mathcal{T}$ry to understand.
Your souls aren't
harmed by what you
eat, but by what you
think and say!

Mark 7:14–16 TLB

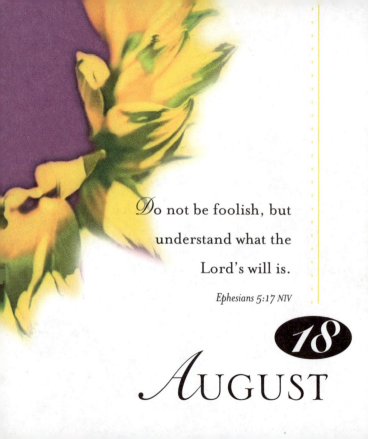

*D*o not be foolish, but understand what the Lord's will is.

Ephesians 5:17 NIV

18
August

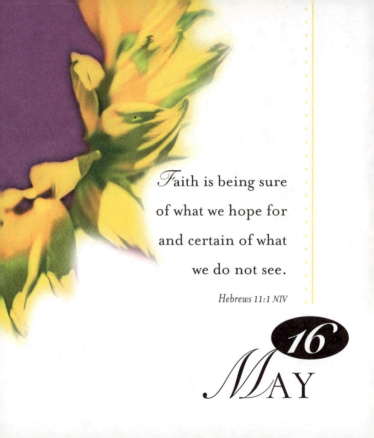

$\mathcal{F}$aith is being sure of what we hope for and certain of what we do not see.

Hebrews 11:1 NIV

$\mathcal{M}$AY 16

The man of few words and settled mind is wise; therefore, even a fool is thought to be wise when he is silent.

Proverbs 17:27-28 TLB

August 17

Develop your business first before building your house.

Proverbs 24:27 TLB

MAY 17

You will return to the ground from which you came. For you were made from the ground, and to the ground you will return.

Genesis 3:19 TLB

16
AUGUST

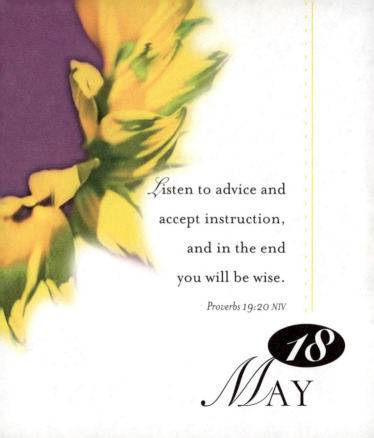

Listen to advice and accept instruction, and in the end you will be wise.

Proverbs 19:20 NIV

MAY 18

O the depth of the riches both of the wisdom and knowledge of God! how unsearchable are his judgments, and his ways past finding out!

Romans 11:33 KJV

15
AUGUST

*N*ever pay back evil for evil. Do things in such a way that everyone can see you are honest clear through.

Romans 12:17 TLB

*M*AY 19

> *No one is like you, O LORD; you are great, and your name is mighty in power.*
>
> *Jeremiah 10:6 NIV*

14 AUGUST

Godliness with contentment is great gain.

1 Timothy 6:6 NIV

MAY **20**

Pray much for others; plead for God's mercy upon them; give thanks for all he is going to do for them.

1 Timothy 2:1 TLB

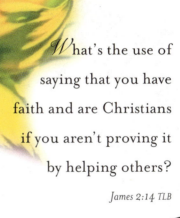

*W*hat's the use of saying that you have faith and are Christians if you aren't proving it by helping others?

James 2:14 TLB

May 21

Much dreaming and many words are meaningless. Therefore stand in awe of God.

Ecclesiastes 5:7 NIV

12
August

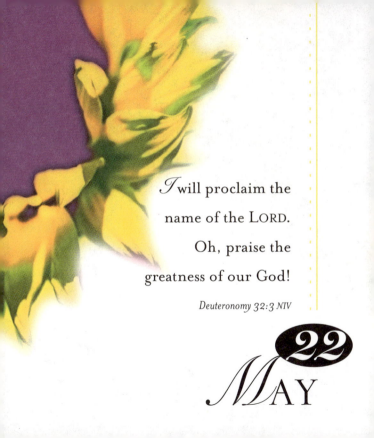

I will proclaim the name of the LORD. Oh, praise the greatness of our God!

Deuteronomy 32:3 NIV

MAY 22

> *You* will call upon me and come and pray to me, and I will listen to you. You will seek me and find me when you seek me with all your heart.
>
> *Jeremiah 29:12-13 NIV*

11
August

> *Return to the LORD your God, for he is gracious and compassionate, slow to anger and abounding in love, and he relents from sending calamity.*
>
> *Joel 2:13 NIV*

May 23

Do nothing out of selfish ambition or vain conceit, but in humility consider others better than yourselves.

Philippians 2:3 NIV

10
August

He who oppresses the poor shows contempt for their Maker, but whoever is kind to the needy honors God.

Proverbs 14:31 NIV

MAY 24

Blessed are all who hear the Word of God and put it into practice.

Luke 11:28 TLB

August 9

My contentment is not in wealth but in seeing you and knowing all is well between us.

Psalm 17:15 TLB

May 25

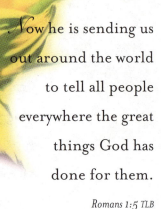

Now he is sending us out around the world to tell all people everywhere the great things God has done for them.

Romans 1:5 TLB

Let us love one another, for love comes from God. Everyone who loves has been born of God and knows God.

1 John 4:7 NIV

MAY 26

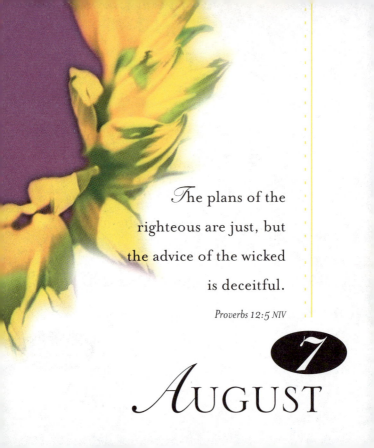

The plans of the righteous are just, but the advice of the wicked is deceitful.

Proverbs 12:5 NIV

7

AUGUST

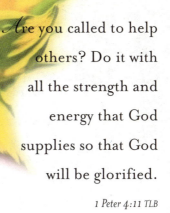

Are you called to help others? Do it with all the strength and energy that God supplies so that God will be glorified.

1 Peter 4:11 TLB

MAY 27

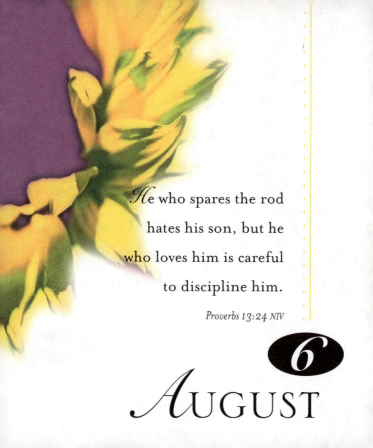

> *He* who spares the rod
> hates his son, but he
> who loves him is careful
> to discipline him.
>
> *Proverbs 13:24 NIV*

6

August

Your conversation should be so sensible and logical that anyone who wants to argue will be ashamed of himself.

Titus 2:8 TLB

May 28

*E*ach believer should confess his sins to God when he is aware of them, while there is time to be forgiven.

Psalm 32:6 TLB

⑤ AUGUST

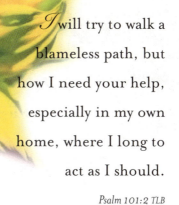

I will try to walk a blameless path, but how I need your help, especially in my own home, where I long to act as I should.

Psalm 101:2 TLB

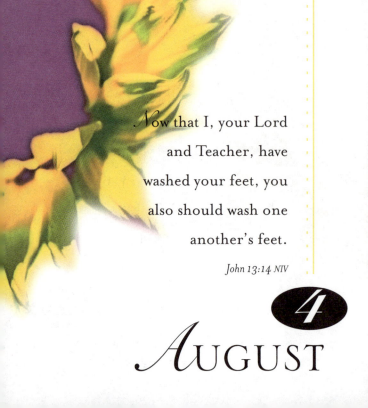

> Now that I, your Lord and Teacher, have washed your feet, you also should wash one another's feet.
>
> *John 13:14 NIV*

4 AUGUST

Give thanks to the LORD, for he is good; his love endures forever.

Psalm 118:29 NIV

30 MAY

Memorial Day

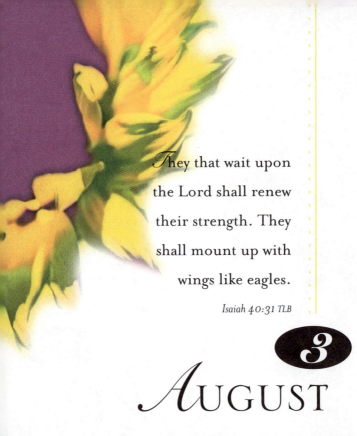

They that wait upon the Lord shall renew their strength. They shall mount up with wings like eagles.

Isaiah 40:31 TLB

3

August

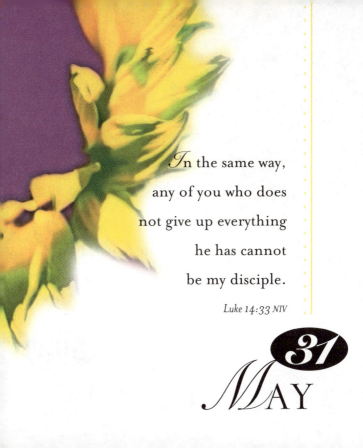

In the same way, any of you who does not give up everything he has cannot be my disciple.

Luke 14:33 NIV

31 MAY

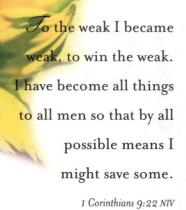

> To the weak I became weak, to win the weak. I have become all things to all men so that by all possible means I might save some.
>
> *1 Corinthians 9:22 NIV*

2 AUGUST

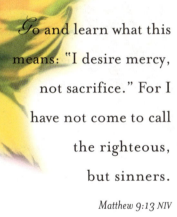

Go and learn what this means: "I desire mercy, not sacrifice." For I have not come to call the righteous, but sinners.

Matthew 9:13 NIV

God says, See, I am placing a Foundation Stone in Zion—a firm, tested, precious Cornerstone that is safe to build on.

Isaiah 28:16 TLB

AUGUST 1

*N*either height nor depth, nor anything else in all creation, will be able to separate us from the love of God that is in Christ Jesus our Lord.

Romans 8:39 NIV

June 2

The Lord your God is the faithful God who for a thousand generations keeps his promises and constantly loves those who love him.

Deuteronomy 7:9 TLB

Surely God is my salvation; I will trust and not be afraid. The LORD, the LORD, is my strength and my song.

Isaiah 12:2 NIV

3
JUNE

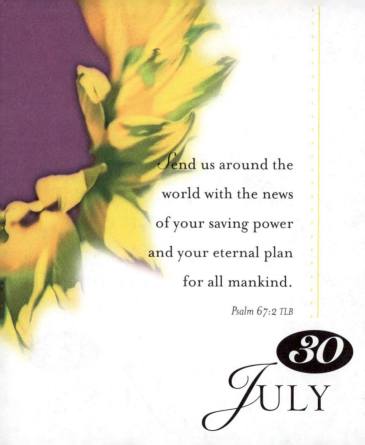

Send us around the world with the news of your saving power and your eternal plan for all mankind.

Psalm 67:2 TLB

30 JULY

The Holy Spirit helps us with our daily problems and in our praying. For we don't even know what we should pray for.

Romans 8:26 TLB

Share with God's people who are in need. Practice hospitality.

Romans 12:13 NIV

29 JULY

It is far better not to say you'll do something than to say you will and then not do it.

Ecclesiastes 5:5 TLB

5 JUNE

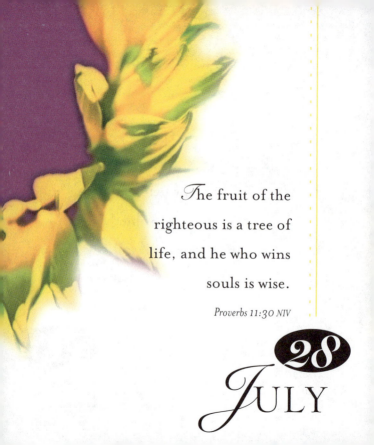

The fruit of the righteous is a tree of life, and he who wins souls is wise.

Proverbs 11:30 NIV

28 JULY

Getting wisdom is the most important thing you can do! And with your wisdom, develop common sense and good judgment.

Proverbs 4:7 TLB

*H*onor the Lord by giving him the first part of all your income.

Proverbs 3:9 TLB

27 JULY

What happiness for those whose guilt has been forgiven! . . . What relief for those who have confessed their sins and God has cleared their record.

Psalm 32:1-2 TLB

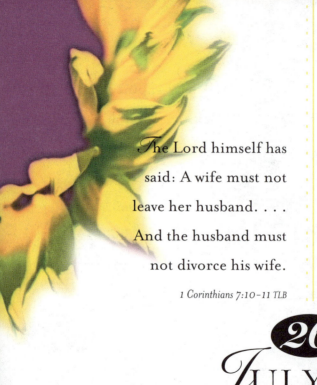

The Lord himself has said: A wife must not leave her husband.... And the husband must not divorce his wife.

1 Corinthians 7:10–11 TLB

26 JULY

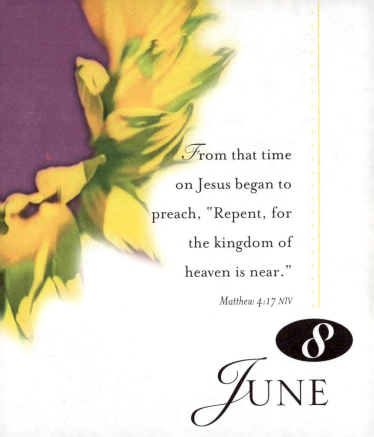

From that time on Jesus began to preach, "Repent, for the kingdom of heaven is near."

Matthew 4:17 NIV

June 8

Drink from your own well, my son—be faithful and true to your wife. . . . Be happy, yes, rejoice in the wife of your youth.

Proverbs 5:15, 18 TLB

> You know that the testing of your faith develops perseverance. Perseverance must finish its work so that you may be mature and complete, not lacking anything.
>
> *James 1:3-4 NIV*

June 9

Let us consider how we may spur one another on toward love and good deeds.

Hebrews 10:24 NIV

24
JULY

A kind man benefits himself, but a cruel man brings trouble on himself.

Proverbs 11:17 NIV

June 10

Yet I am always with you; you hold me by my right hand. You guide me with your counsel, and afterward you will take me into glory.

Psalm 73:23-24 NIV

23 JULY

Love the LORD your God, listen to his voice, and hold fast to him. For the LORD is your life.

Deuteronomy 30:20 NIV

11 JUNE

He who loves money shall never have enough. The foolishness of thinking that wealth brings happiness! The more you have, the more you spend.

Ecclesiastes 5:10–11 TLB

22 JULY

> You will go wherever I send you. . . . Don't be afraid of the people, for I, the Lord, will be with you and see you through.
>
> *Jeremiah 1:7–8 TLB*

12 JUNE

You will keep in perfect peace him whose mind is steadfast, because he trusts in you.

Isaiah 26:3 NIV

21 JULY

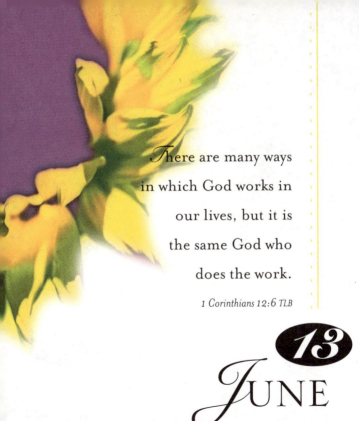

There are many ways in which God works in our lives, but it is the same God who does the work.

1 Corinthians 12:6 TLB

13 JUNE

Take note of this: Everyone should be quick to listen, slow to speak and slow to become angry.

James 1:19 NIV

20

JULY

*W*hen giving your decisions, . . . never favor a man because he is rich; be fair to great and small alike.

Deuteronomy 1:17 TLB

14

*J*UNE

Flag Day

From everyone who has been given much, much will be demanded; and from the one who has been entrusted with much, much more will be asked.

Luke 12:48 NIV

19 JULY

Bear with each other and forgive whatever grievances you may have against one another. Forgive as the Lord forgave you.

Colossians 3:13 NIV

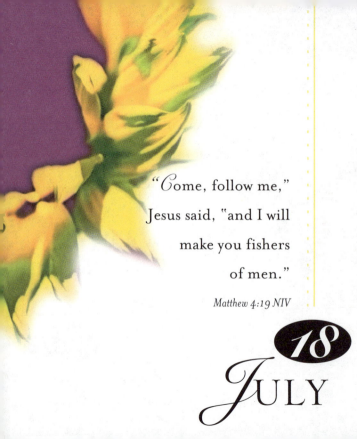

"Come, follow me," Jesus said, "and I will make you fishers of men."

Matthew 4:19 NIV

18
JULY

God has bought you with a great price. So use every part of your body to give glory back to God because he owns it.

1 Corinthians 6:20 TLB

June 16

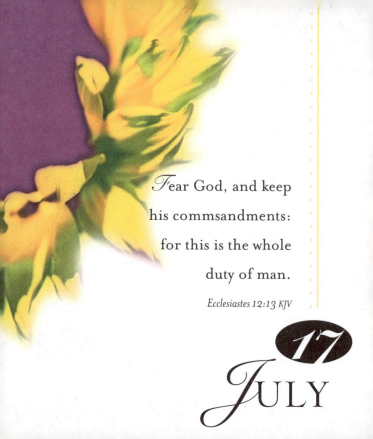

Fear God, and keep his commsandments: for this is the whole duty of man.

Ecclesiastes 12:13 KJV

17 JULY

Oh, turn from your sins while there is yet time. Put them behind you and receive a new heart and a new spirit.

Ezekiel 18:30-31 TLB

17

June

Taste and see that the LORD is good; blessed is the man who takes refuge in him.

Psalm 34:8 NIV

16 JULY

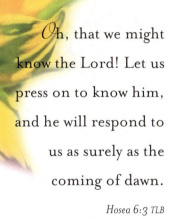

Oh, that we might know the Lord! Let us press on to know him, and he will respond to us as surely as the coming of dawn.

Hosea 6:3 TLB

Cling tightly to your faith in Christ and always keep your conscience clear, doing what you know is right.

1 Timothy 1:19 TLB

15 JULY

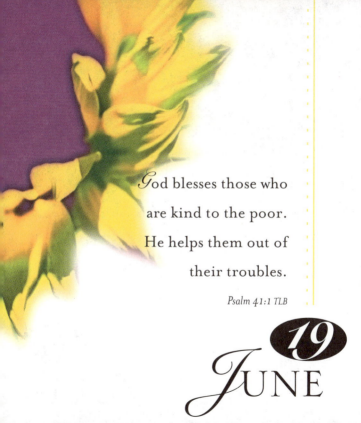

God blesses those who are kind to the poor. He helps them out of their troubles.

Psalm 41:1 TLB

19 JUNE

For the LORD loves the just and will not forsake his faithful ones. They will be protected forever.

Psalm 37:28 NIV

14 JULY

Trust in the LORD with all thine heart; and lean not unto thine own understanding. In all thy ways acknowledge him, and he shall direct thy paths.

Proverbs 3:5-6 KJV

20 JUNE

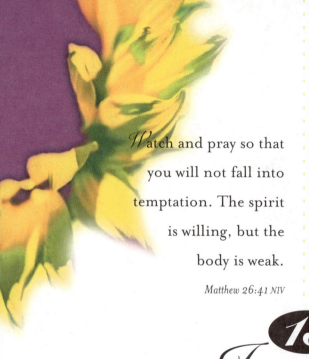

Watch and pray so that you will not fall into temptation. The spirit is willing, but the body is weak.

Matthew 26:41 NIV

Repent and be baptized, every one of you, in the name of Jesus Christ for the forgiveness of your sins. And you will receive the gift of the Holy Spirit.

Acts 2:38 NIV

21 JUNE

The earth shall be filled with the knowledge of the glory of the LORD, as the waters cover the sea.

Habakkuk 2:14 KJV

> This is my prayer:
> that your love may
> abound more and more
> in knowledge and
> depth of insight.
>
> *Philippians 1:9 NIV*

22
JUNE

Jesus told him, "Anyone who lets himself be distracted from the work I plan for him is not fit for the Kingdom of God."

Luke 9:62 TLB

11 JULY

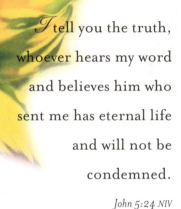

I tell you the truth, whoever hears my word and believes him who sent me has eternal life and will not be condemned.

John 5:24 NIV

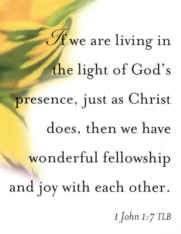

If we are living in the light of God's presence, just as Christ does, then we have wonderful fellowship and joy with each other.

1 John 1:7 TLB

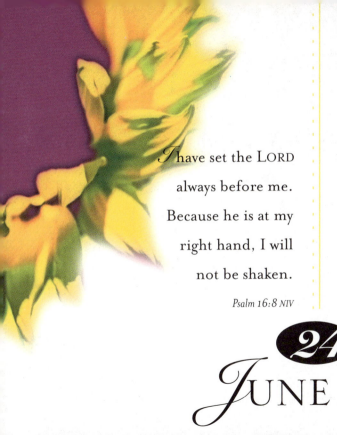

> I have set the LORD always before me. Because he is at my right hand, I will not be shaken.
>
> *Psalm 16:8 NIV*

24 JUNE

Always be joyful.
Always keep on praying.
No matter what happens,
always be thankful,
for this is God's will
for you.

1 Thessalonians 5:16–18 TLB

9 JULY

His delight will be obedience to the Lord. He will not judge by appearance, false evidence, or hearsay, but will defend the poor.

Isaiah 11:3-4 TLB

He who answers before listening—that is his folly and his shame.

Proverbs 18:13 NIV

JULY 8

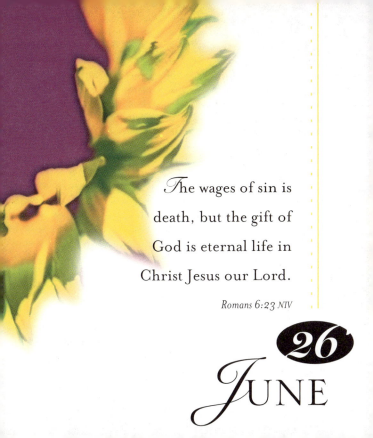

The wages of sin is death, but the gift of God is eternal life in Christ Jesus our Lord.

Romans 6:23 NIV

26 JUNE

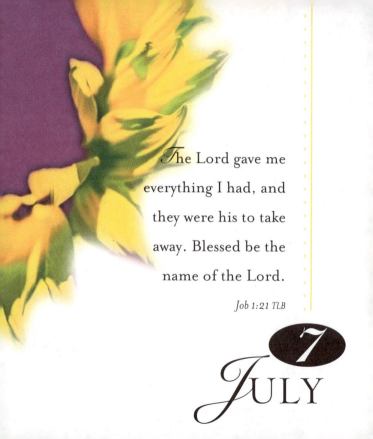

> The Lord gave me everything I had, and they were his to take away. Blessed be the name of the Lord.
>
> *Job 1:21 TLB*

July 7

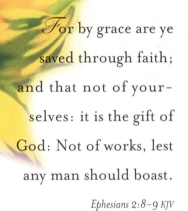

For by grace are ye saved through faith; and that not of yourselves: it is the gift of God: Not of works, lest any man should boast.

Ephesians 2:8-9 KJV

The Lord is in his holy temple; let all the earth be silent before him.

Habakkuk 2:20 NIV

6 JULY

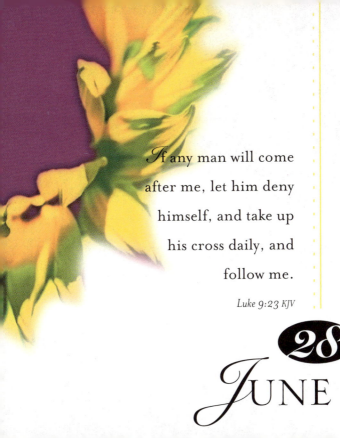

If any man will come after me, let him deny himself, and take up his cross daily, and follow me.

Luke 9:23 KJV

28 JUNE

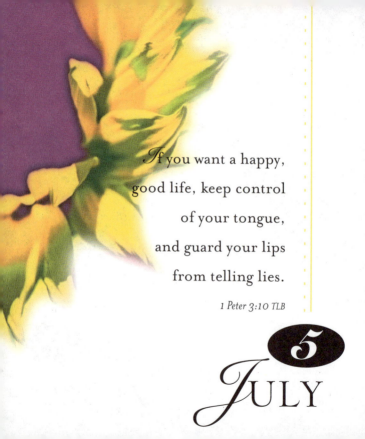

If you want a happy, good life, keep control of your tongue, and guard your lips from telling lies.

1 Peter 3:10 TLB

5 JULY

You are a God of forgiveness, always ready to pardon, gracious and merciful, slow to become angry, and full of love and mercy.

Nehemiah 9:17 TLB

June 29

I have come into the world as a light, so that no one who believes in me should stay in darkness.

John 12:46 NIV

4 JULY
Independence Day

In the morning, O LORD, you hear my voice; in the morning I lay my requests before you and wait in expectation.

Psalm 5:3 NIV

Your attitude must be like my own, for I, the Messiah, did not come to be served, but to serve, and to give my life as a ransom for many.

Matthew 20:28 TLB